Made in the USA
Middletown, DE
19 March 2022

62904982R00057